DRAW
Ocean Animals

by Doug DuBosque

Peel Productions

BOOKS FOR GROWING PEOPLE

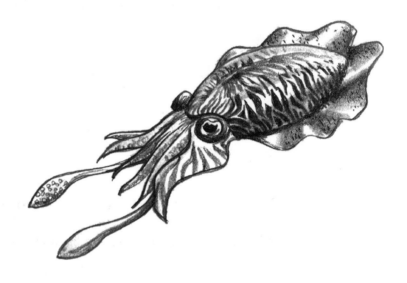

Published by Peel Productions, Inc.
Manufactured in the United States of America

Cataloging-in-Publication Data

DuBosque, D. C.
    Draw ocean animals / by Doug DuBosque
        p.   cm.
        Includes index.
        ISBN 0-939217-24-4
    1. Marine fauna in art--Juvenile literature. 2. Drawing--technique--
Juvenile literature. [1. Marine animals in art. 2. Drawing--Technique.]
I. Title.
NC781.D83 1994
743'.6--dc20
                               94-26897

Distributed to the trade and art
markets in North America by

NORTH LIGHT BOOKS,
an imprint of F&W Publications, Inc.
4700 East Galbraith Road
Cincinnati, OH 45236

(800) 289-0963

Contents

Introduction

Watching ocean animals, and learning about them, creates a sense of delight and awe. Look at how they move, how they hunt and how they hide!

Wouldn't it be great to catch some of that excitement in your own drawings?

This book shows you how, with step by step instructions. You'll be surprised how easy it is to draw, without tracing, a wide range of ocean animals.

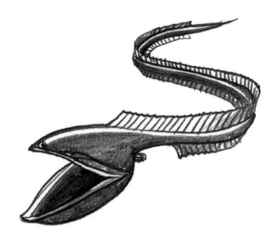

Think of drawing in three steps. The first is getting all the shapes and pieces in the right place. Always draw lightly at first! The second is finishing the drawing–adding details, textures and shading. The final step is 'cleaning up' by erasing the lines you don't need.

In these pages, I will take you through all the steps. The first step will be shown in several drawings, as we draw lightly, putting the pieces together. The final drawing of each set shows a finished drawing, with details and shading added and the 'cleaning up' completed. You can find out more about finishing techniques by looking at the last section of the book, *Drawing Tips*.

I think you'll be surprised by your own great drawings of ocean animals. Putting the pieces together, one step at a time, is much more rewarding than tracing! Have fun looking and learning!

Supplies

- **pencil** (any kind)
- **fine marker** (optional)
- **pencil sharpener**
- **eraser** (I like the kneadable type)
- **paper** (drawing paper erases best)
- **blending stump** if you want to do smooth shading (you can use your finger, too, but it's a bit messy)
- **place to draw**
- **POSITIVE ATTITUDE!**

Sharks and Rays

Always draw lightly at first!

Great White Shark

Carcharodon carcharias.
Size: 6 m (19.5 ft). Diet: fish, seals, dolphins, unlucky humans. Large and aggressive! The great white shark has protective eyelids that cover the eyes during attacks.

1. Draw a long, flat oval. Add a box at one end for the head, and two lines tapering at the other end for the tail.

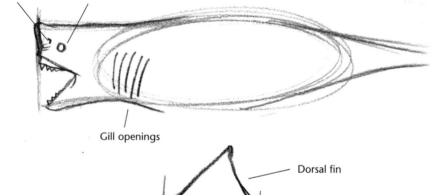

Nostril   Eye

Gill openings

2. Add mouth, teeth, eye, nostril and gill openings.

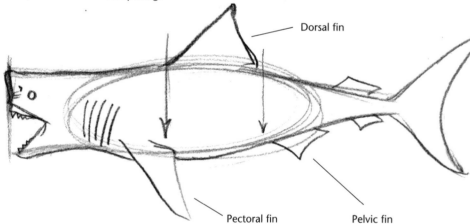

Dorsal fin

Pectoral fin   Pelvic fin

3. Next draw the triangle-shaped dorsal fin on top, behind the center of your oval. Draw the pectoral fin behind the gill openings.

   Draw the pelvic fin. It lies below the back of the dorsal fin. Add the two other small fins. Now draw the tail.

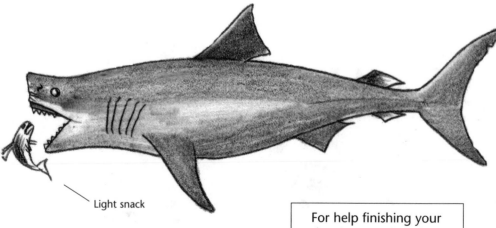

Light snack

4. Add shading. Make the outlines and details bolder. Erase the lines you don't need.

For help finishing your drawing, see *Drawing Tips* on pages 58-62.

Always draw lightly at first!

Shortfin Mako Shark

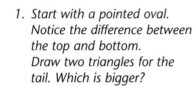

Isurus oxyrhincus.
Size: 3-4 m (10-13 ft). Diet: tuna, mackerel, herring, sardines, squid.

1. *Start with a pointed oval. Notice the difference between the top and bottom. Draw two triangles for the tail. Which is bigger?*

Dorsal fin

2. *Next, draw the dorsal fin, above the middle of the oval.*

   The back of the pectoral fin lines up with the front of the dorsal fin. Draw it.

Pectoral fin

3. *Add gill openings, eye, nostril, mouth and other fins.*

Eye

Mouth

Gill openings

4. *Add shading. Sharpen details (did you catch the notch in the tail?). Clean up with your eraser.*

Thresher Shark

Alopias vulpinus.
Size: 6 m (19.5 ft). Diet: fish. Long tail is used to herd schooling fish, making them easier to catch.

1. Draw an oval with pointed ends. Add the tail. Make it as long as the body.

Tail

2. Add the dorsal fin above the middle of the body.

   Carefully look at the top and bottom part of the tail. Now draw them, lightly at first.

Dorsal fin

3. Add the other fins and details. Pay close attention to the spatial relationships (in other words, put things in the right places)!

Gill openings

Pectoral fin

Pelvic fin

5. Add shading. Sharpen lines and details. Clean up any smudges with your eraser.

   Cool looking shark!

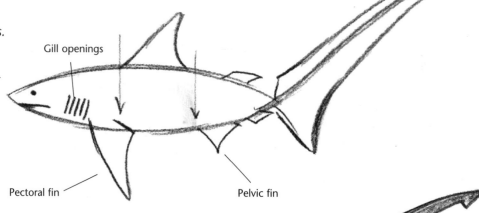

For help finishing your drawing, see *Drawing Tips* on pages 58-62.

Always draw lightly at first!

Sand Tiger

Odontaspis taurus.
Size: 3.2 m (10.5 ft) Diet: fish. Lives at the bottom of shallow waters.

1. Draw a long, flat oval with an extending point at one end for the head, and a long, bending point at the other for the tail.

Gill openings

Pectoral fin

2. Draw the mouth and eye. Add gill openings and pectoral fin.

3. Look at the tail fin. Draw it, lightly at first! Add the other fins, all about the same size as one another.

Tail fin

Second dorsal fin

First dorsal fin

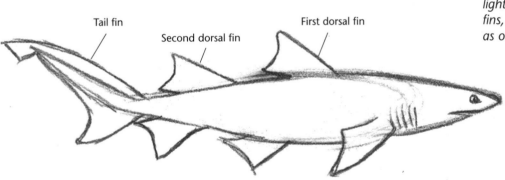

4. Add shading. Sharpen outlines and details. Clean up any smudges with your eraser.

Hammerhead Shark

Sphyrna mokarran (Great hammerhead). Size: 6m (19.5 ft) Diet: fish, especially rays. With eyes facing out to the side, hammerheads have to turn from side to side as they swim.

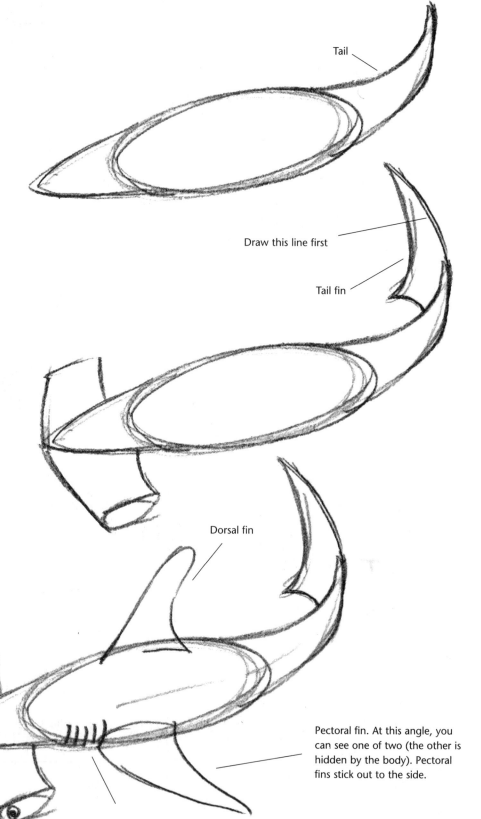

Tail

Draw this line first

Tail fin

Dorsal fin

Pectoral fin. At this angle, you can see one of two (the other is hidden by the body). Pectoral fins stick out to the side.

Eye

Gill openings

1. Start with a tilted oval. Add a curving triangle for the tail, and a pointed end for the head.

2. Look at the curved tail fin. Draw it. Now look at the angle of the head. Draw it carefully, paying attention to angles.

3. Add the one eye you can see from this angle. Draw gill openings. Next add the pectoral and dorsal fins.

Always draw lightly at first!

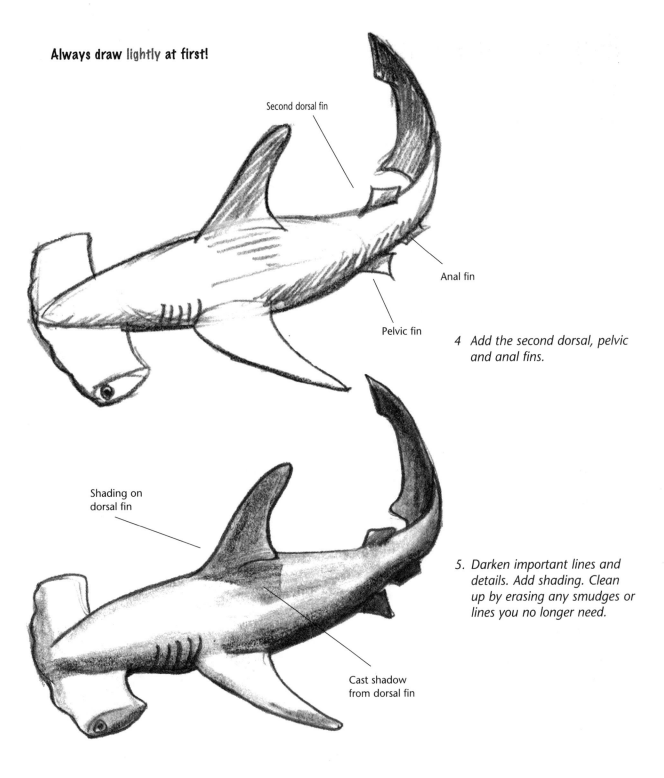

Second dorsal fin

Anal fin

Pelvic fin

4 Add the second dorsal, pelvic and anal fins.

Shading on dorsal fin

Cast shadow from dorsal fin

5. Darken important lines and details. Add shading. Clean up by erasing any smudges or lines you no longer need.

Profile view of a Hammerhead shark, showing the shape of the tail more clearly. Scientists don't know why the head is that shape. Some think the winglike shape helps keep the shark swimming level.

Whale Shark

Rhincodon typus.
Size: 15.2 m (50 ft). Diet: small fish, plankton. Filter feeder (notice the very large gill openings). The projections on the front of its mouth are not teeth. It's huge, but a very gentle shark.

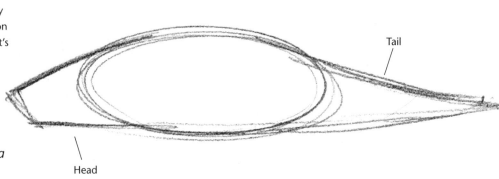

Tail

Head

1. Draw a long, flat oval. Add a slanted box at one end. for the head. Draw a long triangle at the other end for the tail.

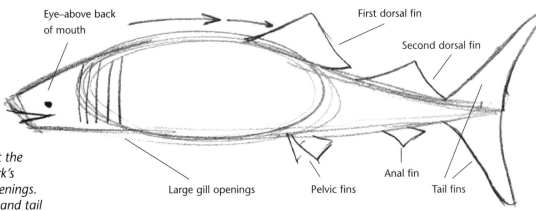

Eye–above back of mouth

First dorsal fin

Second dorsal fin

Large gill openings

Pelvic fins

Anal fin

Tail fins

2. Draw the dorsal fins at the back of the whale shark's body. Add large gill openings. Draw the pelvic, anal, and tail fins. Add the mouth and eye.

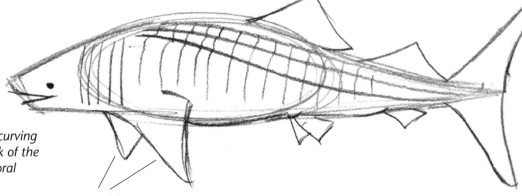

3. Next draw long ridges curving down the side and back of the shark's body. Add pectoral fins.

Pectoral fins

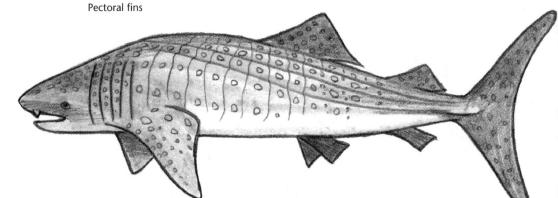

4. Add shading and patterns. Erase smudges and 'leftover' lines.

Always draw lightly at first!

Basking Shark

Cetorhinus maximus.
Size: 10.4 m (34 ft). Diet: plankton.
Filter feeder. Swims along with its
mouth wide open to catch plankton.

1. Draw a flat oval. Draw a box
   at one end, and a triangle at
   the other. A backward 'S'
   curve forms the head.

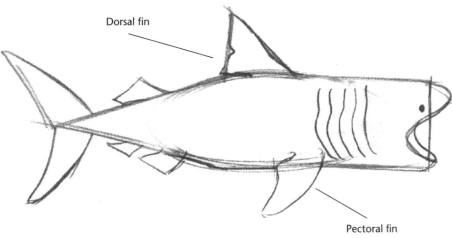

Caudal (tail) fin

Eye

Gill openings

2. Draw the eye and open
   mouth. Draw very large gill
   openings. Draw the caudal
   (tail) fin. Erase parts of the
   oval that you no longer need.

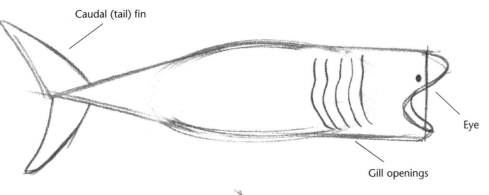

Dorsal fin

Pectoral fin

3. Put the dorsal fin above the
   middle of the oval. Draw the
   pectoral and remaining fins.

4. Finally, add shading and
   sharpen details. Clean up any
   smudges.

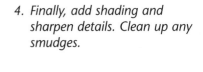

For help finishing your
drawing, see *Drawing
Tips* on pages 58-62.

Port Jackson Shark

Heterodontus portusjacksoni.
Size: up to 1.5 m (5 ft). Diet: probably
mollusks, sea urchins and mollusks;
feeds at night. Has stout spines in front
of each dorsal fin.

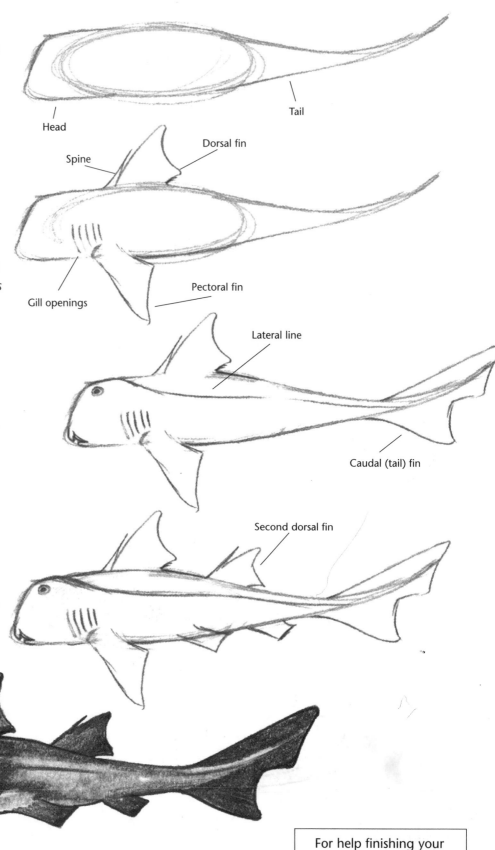

Head

Tail

1. Draw a long, flat oval with a
   rat-like tail. Add a slanting
   box shape for the head.

Spine

Dorsal fin

2. At the front of the oval, draw
   gill openings and the pectoral
   fin. Add the dorsal fin, with its
   pointed spine in the front.

Gill openings

Pectoral fin

Lateral line

3. Draw the eye high in the
   head. Draw the mouth, quite
   unlike other sharks'. Carefully
   add the caudal (tail) fin, and
   the lateral line.

Caudal (tail) fin

4. Draw the second dorsal fin,
   and the fins on the bottom.

Second dorsal fin

5. Add shading. Sharpen
   outlines and details. Clean up
   with your eraser.

For help finishing your
drawing, see *Drawing
Tips* on pages 58-62.

Always draw lightly at first!

Sting Ray

Family *dasayatidae.* Size: 1.5 m (5 ft). Diet: Mollusks and crustaceans on the seabed. Graceful swimmers who live on sandy and muddy bottoms. The sharp spine can be used as a weapon. There are about a hundred species.

1. Start with a box shape. Add the pointed tail with its spine. This is where the 'sting' in stingray comes from.

Spiracle

Gill opening

2. Make the outline wiggly. Add eyes, gills and spiracles, which are where the ray breathes in (its mouth is on the bottom; it breathes out through its gills). Carefully erase your straight lines.

3 Sharpen outlines and details. Add the little lines around the outside. Add shading. Clean up any smudges with your eraser.

Atlantic Manta

Manta birostris.
Size: up to 6.7m (27ft) wide. Diet: plankton, fish and crustaceans. The 'hands' on either side of the mouth can be extended, or used as scoops to direct food into the mouth.

1. Draw a big, swooping curve.

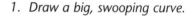

2. Add a bump in the middle.

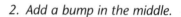

3. Next draw an arching curve to make one 'wing.'

4. Lightly draw in a 'C' shape for the projections at either side of the mouth.

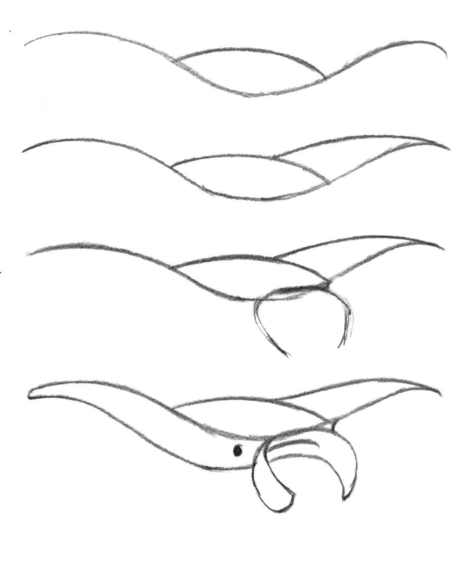

5. Add a line for the bottom of the closer wing. Draw the eye. Look carefully at my example to see how to finish the mouth.

6. Add the tail. Sharpen outlines, add shading, and clean up any smudges with your eraser.

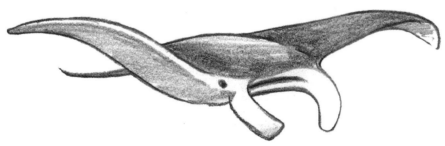

Whales & Other Mammals

Always draw lightly at first!

Sperm Whale

Physeter catodon.
Size: 11-20 m (36-66 ft). Diet: mainly
large, deepwater squid.

1. Draw a long rectangle.

2. Add one big triangle and two
   small triangles for the tail
   flukes.

Tail fluke

Tail fluke

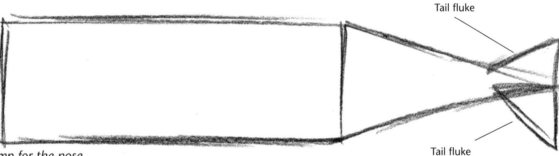

3. Draw a bump for the nose,
   and a long line for the mouth.
   Add the eye, and small flipper.

Eye

Flipper

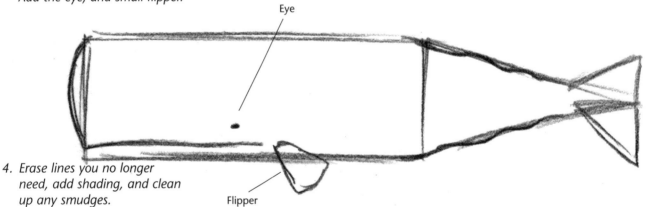

4. Erase lines you no longer
   need, add shading, and clean
   up any smudges.

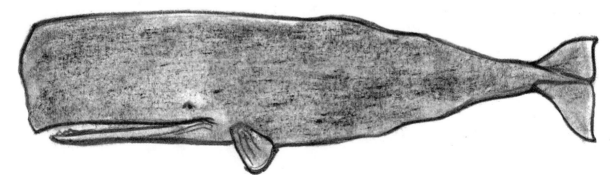

Always draw lightly at first!

White (Beluga) Whale

Delphinapterus leucas.
Size: 4-6 m (13-20 ft). Diet: fish and crustaceans from the sea bottom. White whales sing a variety of songs. Nineteenth century whalers called them sea canaries.

Tail

1. *Draw a large, flat oval with another oval overlapping it. Add a triangular projection at the other end for the tail.*

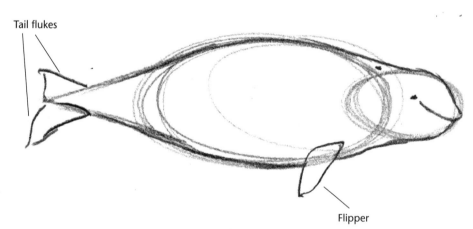

Tail flukes

Flipper

2. *Add two small triangles for the tail flukes. Draw the flipper on the lower front of the big oval. Draw the mouth upward like a smile. Add the eye.*

3. *Erase what's left of the ovals. Go over outlines. This whale is very light in color, so there's not much shading to do. Clean up any smudges with your eraser.*

Blow hole

Easy, eh?

For help finishing your drawing, see *Drawing Tips* on pages 58-62.

Blue Whale

Balaenoptera musculus.
Size: 25-32 m (82-105 ft). Diet: plankton. Strains food through the baleen plates attached to upper jaw. The largest mammal that has ever existed. Feeds in polar waters during summer months, eating four tons of tiny shrimp each day. Migrates to warmer waters to breed. Endangered.

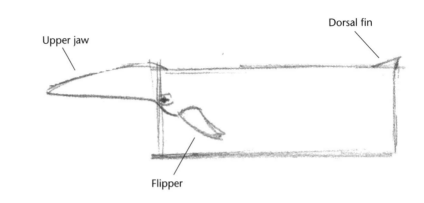

Upper jaw

Dorsal fin

Flipper

1. Draw a long rectangle. Add the little dorsal fin. Add the eye. Draw the flipper. Add the upper jaw.

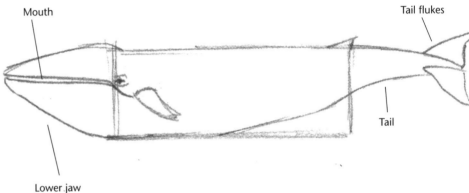

Mouth

Tail flukes

Tail

Lower jaw

2. Taper the bottom of the whale's body upward, and extend it to form the tail. Extend the top line of the rectangle to meet it. Add the tail flukes. Draw the lower jaw, leaving space to show the baleen plates in the mouth.

4. Erase parts of the rectangle you no longer need, and go over the outline. Add the grooves on the lower jaw.

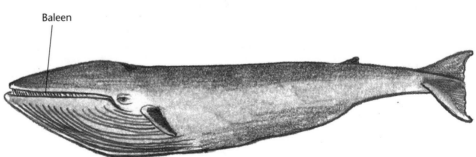

Baleen

5. Add shading. Sharpen outlines and details (notice the baleen plates visible in the mouth). Clean up with your eraser.

Always draw lightly at first!

Gray Whale

Eschrichtius robustus.
Size: 12-15 m (40-50 ft). Diet: planktonic shrimp, which it stirs up from the bottom, unlike other whales. Strains food through the baleen plates attached to upper jaw.

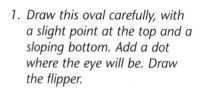

Eye

Flipper

1. Draw this oval carefully, with a slight point at the top and a sloping bottom. Add a dot where the eye will be. Draw the flipper.

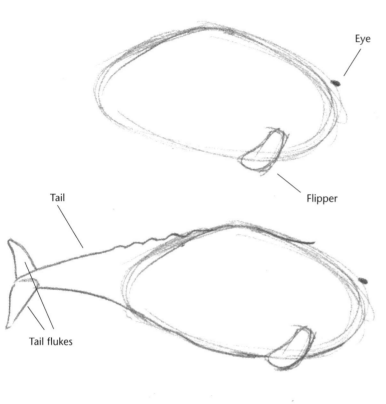

Tail

Tail flukes

2. Draw the tail, with bumps. Add tail flukes.

3. Add the head, with a bump on the top. Draw a line for the mouth.

Mouth

4. Add shading. Sharpen outlines and details. Clean up any smudges with your eraser.

For help finishing your drawing, see *Drawing Tips* on pages 58-62.

Minke Whale

Balaenoptera acutorostrata.
Size: 8-10 m (26-33 ft). Diet: plankton, fish, squid. Strains food through the baleen plates attached to upper jaw.

1. Draw a long, slightly curving line for the back. Add a curved line under it.

2. Draw the small dorsal fin. Add the small, rounded flipper. Add a slight bump at the head. Extend the bottom curved line upward to form the tail. Add tail flukes. Erase the part of the curve you no longer need.

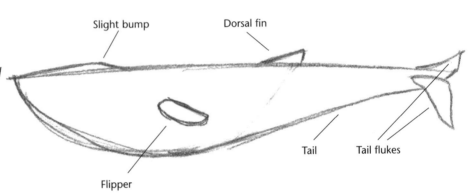

Slight bump   Dorsal fin

Tail   Tail flukes

Flipper

3. The mouth is at the top of the head, and turns down at the back. Draw the mouth, and the eye at the back of it. Draw the grooves on the lower jaw. You may find it easier to draw these with your paper upside down.

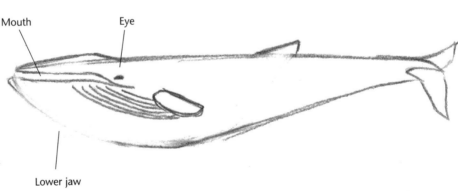

Mouth   Eye

Lower jaw

4. Now, sharpen outlines and details. Add shading. Clean up any smudges with your eraser.

Baleen plates

For help finishing your drawing, see *Drawing Tips* on pages 58-62.

Always draw lightly at first!

Humpback Whale

Megaptera novaeangliae.
Size: 14.6-19m (48-62 ft). Diet: plankton and fish. Strains food through the baleen plates attached to upper jaw. Many knobs and barnacles on body and very long flippers. Feeds in polar waters in the summer, and migrates to tropical waters for the winter. Endangered.

Tail

Top of head

1. Draw a tilted oval. At the high end, make a curving-down triangle for the tail.

2 Draw the top of the head.

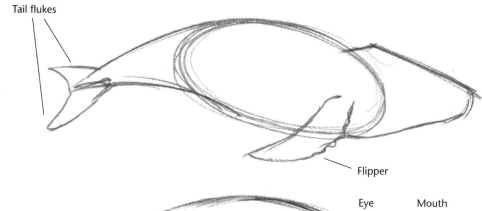

Tail flukes

Flipper

3. Add the bottom of the head. Add a long, slightly curving flipper with one bumpy side. Draw two triangle shapes for the tail flukes.

4. Add a line for the mouth. Draw the eye. Add curved lines on the lower jaw. Add bumps and barnacles on the head and flipper.

Eye   Mouth

Dorsal fin

Lower jaw

5. Draw the dorsal fin. Add shading. Sharpen outlines and details. Clean up any smudges with your eraser.

Great whale!

Listen to a recording of humpback whales singing sometime....

Bowhead Whale

Balaena mysticetus.
Size: 15-20 m (49-66 ft). Diet: plankton. The large vertical lines in the mouth are baleen, with which the whale strains plankton out of the water as it swims. *Endangered.*

1. Draw a box. Add three curving triangle shapes for the tail and tail flukes.

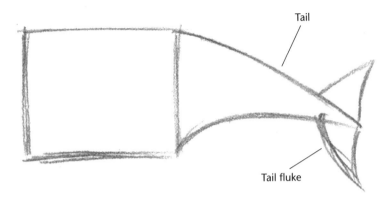

Tail

Tail fluke

2. Draw the upper jaw. Notice where the line for the mouth and the box intersect. Add the eye.

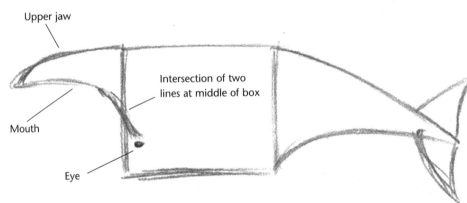

Upper jaw

Intersection of two lines at middle of box

Mouth

Eye

3. Draw the flipper, then the bottom of the mouth, lower jaw, and baleen plates. Draw lightly and take your time! Add the flipper. Add the bump on top.

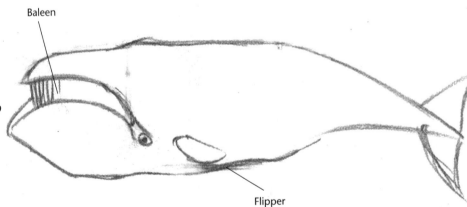

Baleen

Flipper

4. Add shading. Sharpen outlines and details. Clean up any smudges with your eraser.

For help finishing your drawing, see *Drawing Tips* on pages 58-62.

Killer Whale (male)

Orcinus orca.
Size: 7-9.7 m (23-32 ft). Diet: fish, squid, sea lions, birds. Males have the distinctive dorsal fin (smaller and curved on females and juveniles). Killer whales are black on top, and white on the bottom. Each has a unique pattern.

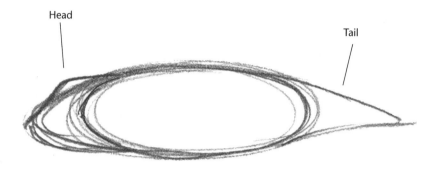

Head
Tail

1. Draw a long, flat oval. Add a triangle for the tail. Draw the head, with a bump on top.

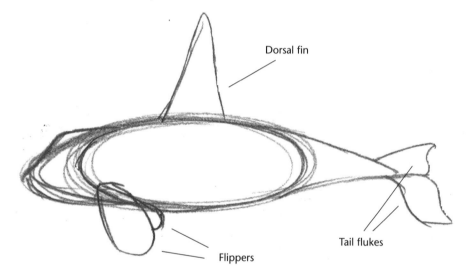

Dorsal fin

Flippers

Tail flukes

2. Draw a very tall dorsal fin on top. Add flippers and tail flukes.

3. Because of their strong black and white coloring, you may want to finish your drawing in ink or marker. Then you can carefully erase pencil lines.

Atlantic Bottlenose Dolphin

Tursiops truncatus.
Size: 4 m (12 ft). Diet: fish. Highly
intelligent animals who live in groups.
These are the dolphins you usually see
in movies or on TV.

1. *Draw a crescent shape.*

2. *Add a pointed nose, and two
   triangles for the tail flukes.
   Add the curved line on the
   side, and the eye.*

3. *Draw the flippers (you only
   see part of the far one, which
   I've shaded) and the dorsal
   fin.*

4. *Make your dolphin jumping
   out of the water if you like.
   Add shading. Sharpen
   outlines and details. Clean up
   any smudges with your eraser.*

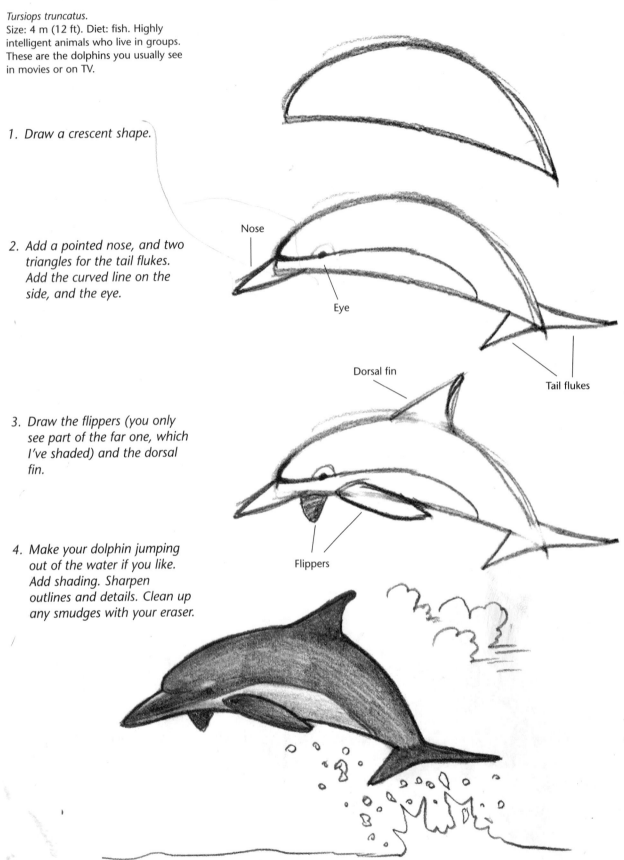

Nose

Eye

Dorsal fin

Tail flukes

Flippers

Always draw lightly at first!

Harbor Porpoise

Phocoena phocoena.
Size: 1.5-1.8 m (5-6 ft). Diet: fish.
Harbor porpoises live in groups and
'talk' a lot. They can dive for up to six
minutes, using clicking sounds and
echolocation to find their prey.

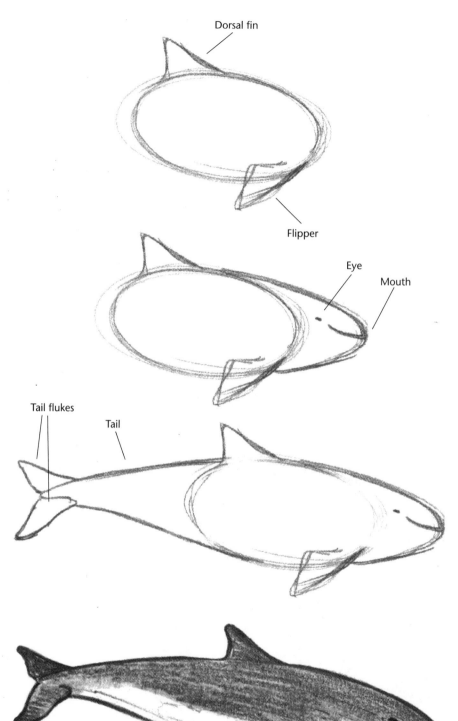

Dorsal fin

Flipper

Eye

Mouth

Tail flukes

Tail

1. Start with an oval. Add the flipper at one end, and the dorsal fin at the other.

2. Extend the oval to form the head. Draw the mouth and eye.

3. Add the tail and tail flukes. Erase unneeded lines .

4. Add shading. Sharpen outlines and details. Clean up with your eraser.

For help finishing your
drawing, see *Drawing
Tips* on pages 58-62.

California Sea Lion

Zalophus californianus.
Size: 6 ft (1.8 m). Diet: fish, octopus, and squid. Unlike seals, sea lions can turn their rear flippers forward, which helps them move on land. Sea lions have ear flaps; seals don't.

1. Draw three tilted ovals. Look carefully at how, and where they connect. Also look at how they tilt.

2. Draw the forward-facing rear flippers and the front flipper. Connect the two largest ovals.

3. Draw the head, and lines to connect it to the middle oval. Add the ear, nostril, eye and whiskers.

4. Now add shading. Notice how I use short strokes of the pencil to suggest fur. Sharpen outlines and details. Clean up any smudges with your eraser.

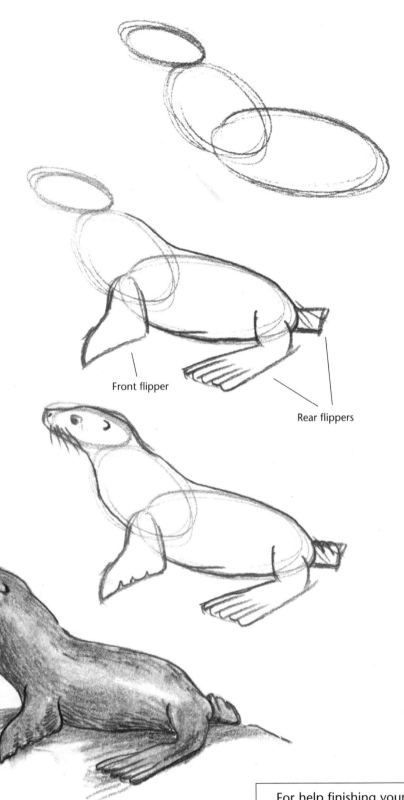

Front flipper

Rear flippers

For help finishing your drawing, see *Drawing Tips* on pages 58-62.

Harbor Seal

Phoca vitulina.
Size: 5 ft (1.5 m). Diet: fish, squid, and crustaceans caught on 4-5 minute dives. Colors vary from light gray to dark brown or black. They come out of the water to spend much of their time on rocks. Unlike sea lions, seals' rear flippers do not turn forward. Seals have no ear flaps.

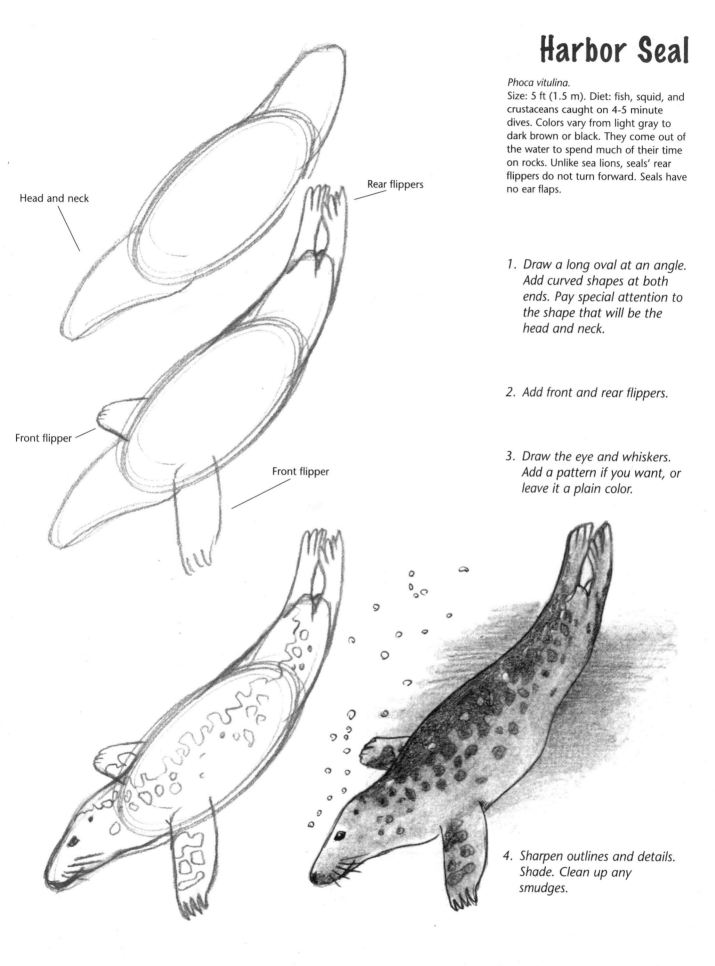

Head and neck

Rear flippers

Front flipper

Front flipper

1. Draw a long oval at an angle. Add curved shapes at both ends. Pay special attention to the shape that will be the head and neck.

2. Add front and rear flippers.

3. Draw the eye and whiskers. Add a pattern if you want, or leave it a plain color.

4. Sharpen outlines and details. Shade. Clean up any smudges.

Northern Elephant Seal

Mirounga angustirostris.
Size: males up to 6m (20 ft), females up to 3m (10 ft). Diet: fish and squid, caught on long, deep dives. Breed on offshore islands; were hunted almost to extinction but have recovered. Unlike sea lions, seals' rear flippers do not turn forward. Seals have no ear flaps.

1. Draw two ovals for the body. Extend both ends with partial ovals.

2. Connect the shapes to make the outline of the seal, with wrinkles. Draw flippers, front and back.

3. Carefully draw the head with its distinctive bulge, mouth and eye (sideways in this posture).

4. Add shading. Sharpen outlines and details. Clean up any smudges with your eraser.

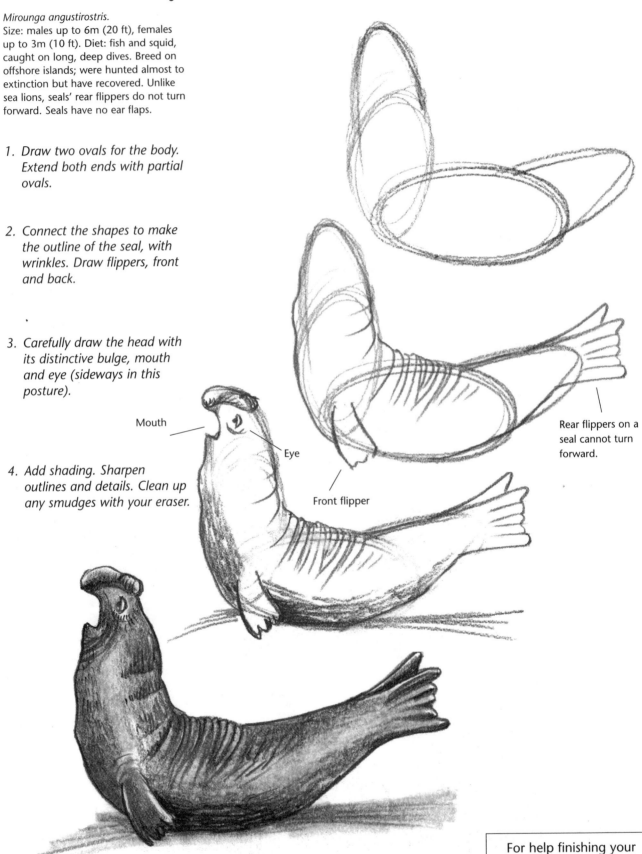

Mouth

Eye

Front flipper

Rear flippers on a seal cannot turn forward.

For help finishing your drawing, see *Drawing Tips* on pages 58-62.

Always draw lightly at first!

Walrus

Odobenus rosmarus.
Size: males 2.7-3.5 m (9-11.5 ft);
females a bit smaller. Diet: mollusks,
crustaceans, starfish, fish. They dive to
feed, and use their tusks to help pick
up food from the sea bottom.

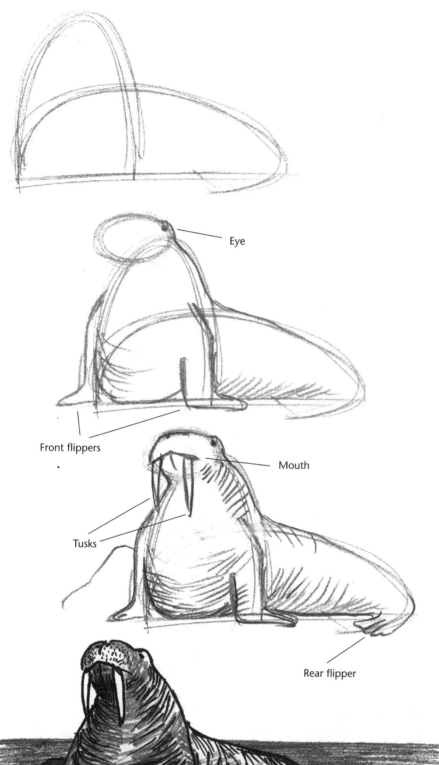

Eye

Front flippers

Tusks

Mouth

Rear flipper

1. Start with two simple shapes.

2. Add an oval for the head.
   Connect the back of the head
   in a smooth curve to the
   back. Draw the eye. Add the
   front flippers.

3. Draw mouth and tusks. Add
   wrinkles. Since the walrus has
   many wrinkles, you can use
   them to make the animal look
   more round (see Drawing
   Tips at the end of the book
   for ideas about drawing with
   contour lines).

4. Add shading. Sharpen
   outlines and details. Clean up
   any smudges with your eraser.
   I finished this drawing by
   going over key lines with a
   fine tip marker.

Manatee

Trichecus manatus (American manatee).
Size: up to 3m (10ft). Diet: mainly
vegetation, found at night by touch
and smell. Manatees sleep in shallow
waters, coming to the surface every
few minutes to breathe–without even
waking up!

1. Draw two overlapping ovals.

2. Add lines for wrinkles at the
   neck, and lines for the tail.

Tail

3. Draw the mouth and face.
   Add the rest of the tail and
   flipper.

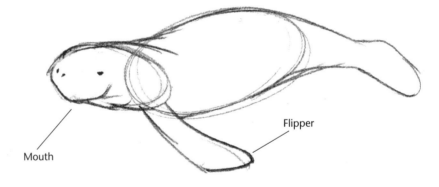

Mouth

Flipper

4. Add shading. Sharpen
   outlines and details. Clean up
   any smudges with your eraser.

ZZZ...

For help finishing your
drawing, see *Drawing
Tips* on pages 58-62.

Coral Reef Animals
Always draw lightly at first!

Parrotfish

Scarus guacamaia (Rainbow Parrotfish). Size: 1.2 m (4 ft). Diet: Algae and coral, which it scrapes off reefs with a parrot-like beak. Like some other parrotfish species, this one can create a mucus 'sleeping bag' around itself at night to protect it from predators.

1. Start with a long oval. Add a point at one end and a rounded shape for a tail at the other.

Tail

2. Add the dorsal fin. Next draw the pectoral fin. Add the pelvic, anal and tail fins.

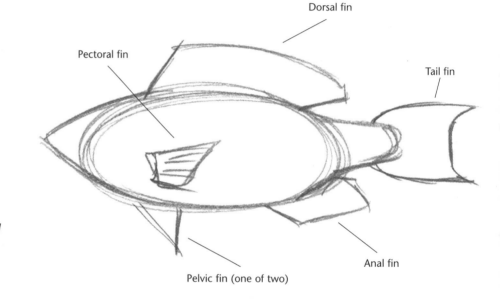

Dorsal fin

Pectoral fin

Tail fin

Pelvic fin (one of two)

Anal fin

3. Draw the mouth, eye, and gill openings. Add scales, spines in the fins, and shading. Sharpen outlines and details. Clean up any smudges with your eraser.

Gill openings

Always draw lightly at first!

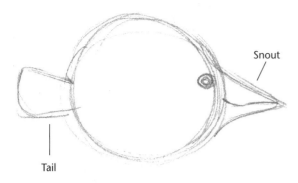

Snout

Tail

Butterflyfish

Chelmon rostratus (copperband or beaked butterflyfish). Size: 20 cm (7.5 in). Diet: small plants and animals that it pulls out of crevices in coral. The big spot on the tail is probably to fool predators into thinking it's the eye. the eye itself is partially camouflaged by the stripe running through it.

1. *Start with a light circle. At one end, in the middle, add the tail. At the other end, draw the long beaklike snout. Add a line for the mouth. Draw the eye.*

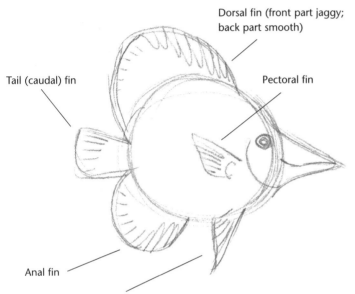

Dorsal fin (front part jaggy; back part smooth)

Tail (caudal) fin

Pectoral fin

Anal fin

Pelvic fin (one of two)

2. *Your next challenge is to draw all the fins with spines. Five fins are visible in this drawing. Draw them all!*

3. *Next, add the camouflage pattern, including the second 'eye' to fool attackers.*

4. *Darken the patterns. The eye and band on the tail are black. The stripes are copper-colored. Sharpen outlines and details. Clean up with your eraser.*

For help finishing your drawing, see *Drawing Tips* on pages 58-62.

Draw Ocean Animals 35

Lionfish

Pterois volitans.
Size: 38 cm (15 in). Lives in the Pacific and Indian Oceans. This is a "look but don't touch!" fish. Colorful fins conceal poisonous spines that will kill other fish and even people. Bright orange and reddish colors make this a very pretty fish. Just don't touch!

1. Start with a simple oval shape. Add a rounded part for the tail at one end, and a point at the other. Draw the eye. Notice where it lies on the oval.

2. Add a line for the mouth, barbels on the chin, and the 'eyebrow' above the eye. Lightly draw radiating curved lines for the spines of the pectoral fin.

3. Complete the pectoral fin. Add the caudal (tail) fin and anal fin. Erase any body lines you no longer need.

4. Add the large dorsal fin, which is in many parts. At the front of each is a spine.

5. To sharpen the lines, you can go over outlines and important details with a fine marker. Clean up with your eraser.

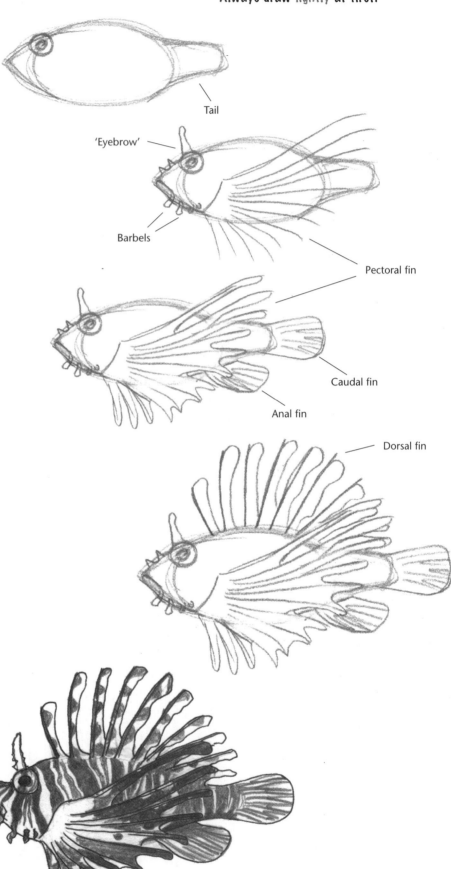

Tail

'Eyebrow'

Barbels

Pectoral fin

Caudal fin

Anal fin

Dorsal fin

Clown Anenome Fish

Amphiprion percula.
Size: 6 cm (2.25 in). Diet: tiny crustaceans and other organisms. Lives in safety amidst the tentacles of sea anenomes, which kill other fish.

Tail

1. *Start with an oval. Add a rounded part at one end for the head. Draw a large eye and the mouth. Notice that the eye touches the outside of the oval. Add the tail.*

2. *Draw top and bottom fins in line with each other.*

3. *Add tentacles of the sea anenome, with some in front of the fish. Lightly erase lines they cross at the bottom of the fish.*

4. *Draw the bold pattern (orange, black and white if you're drawing in color). Add shading. Sharpen outlines and details. Clean up any smudges with your eraser.*

For help finishing your drawing, see *Drawing Tips* on pages 58-62.

Moray Eel

Mureana helena.
Size: 90 cm (35.5 in)
Diet: fish, squid, cuttlefish
Hides in rock or coral crevices, waiting
to lunge at prey swimming by.

This drawing involves depth, and it's a bit more complicated. For that reason, I've broken it down to one line at a time.

1. *Start with a curvy line.*

2. *Add straight vertical lines at the ends and the curves. Hold your pencil flat on the paper if you have trouble seeing how to draw the vertical lines. Add more curved lines beneath the first ones, connecting to the vertical lines. See how you can turn it into a ribbon?*

3. *You may need a couple of tries to figure out the next few steps, so draw lightly at first! Pay special attention to the arrows.*

   From the left side of the ribbon, draw a sausage shape, with your line ending at the arrow.

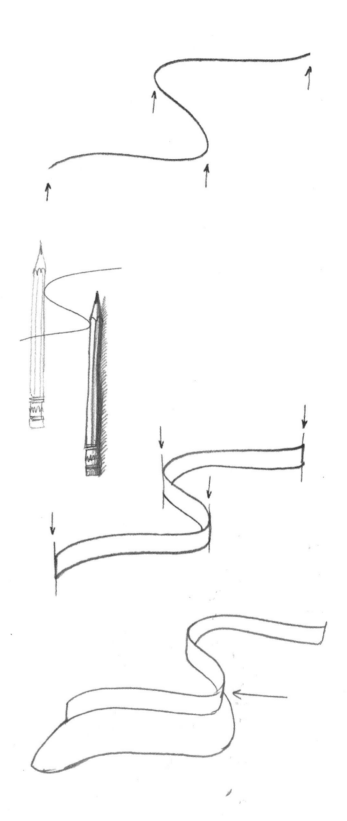

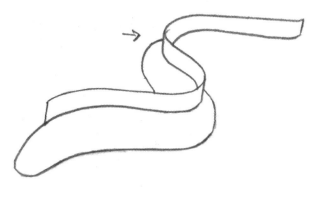

4. Draw a small line to make the second part of the body...

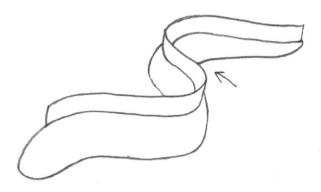

5. Add a third line. Now you've drawn the entire body of the eel. Take a moment to look at your drawing. Does it look like it's swimming toward you?

Cool!

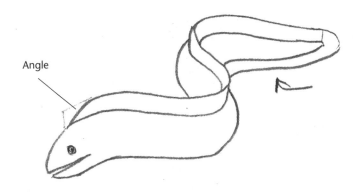

Angle

5. Next add the ribbon-like fin along the bottom of the eel. Draw the mouth and eye. Add an angle to the front of the dorsal fin.

6. Add shading and spots. See Drawing Tips at the end of the book for help with the pattern. Clean up any smudges with your eraser.

For help finishing your drawing, see *Drawing Tips* on pages 58-62.

Queen Triggerfish

Balistes vetula.
Size: 33 cm (13 in). Diet: various invertebrates, primarily sea urchins. 'Trigger' in its name refers to the second dorsal spine, which can be locked against the first dorsal spine. The Triggerfish does this when alarmed, wedging itself in a crevice so that it's almost impossible to get out. When the 'trigger' spine is lowered, the fish swims out again.

1. *Draw a tilted oval. Add the jaws and mouth. Extend the bottom jaw to make the body slightly pointed at the bottom. Draw a small shape for the base of the tail.*

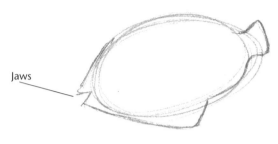

Jaws

2. *Draw the eye—notice how far back it is from the mouth. Add the pectoral fin. Draw the first dorsal fin with spines. Behind it, draw the long pointed second dorsal fin.*

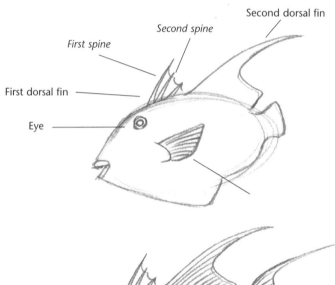

First spine
Second spine
Second dorsal fin
First dorsal fin
Eye

3. *Draw the tail (caudal) fin and the anal fin. Erase parts of the oval you no longer need.*

Caudal (tail) fin
Anal fin

4. *Add stripes, patterns on fins, scales and other details. Clean up any smudges with your eraser.*

The Queen triggerfish has tipped over a sea urchin by blowing a jet of water at it. Now it can attack the soft underside. Its eyes are protected by their distance from the mouth.

For help finishing your drawing, see *Drawing Tips* on pages 58-62.

Always draw lightly at first!

Crown-of-thorns Starfish

Acanthaster planci (Crown-of-thorns starfish). Size: up to 40 cm (16 in) across. Diet: coral. In the mid-1960's, population of this starfish started growing, and large areas of some of the world's coral reefs have been destroyed. Was it because collectors killed too many Triton snails for their shells? Scientists don't know.

Charonia (Triton snail). This snail, whose shell is prized by collectors, feeds on the Crown of Thorns by spearing it with poison, then eating it.

This starfish is making its way slowly across a coral reef, killing coral. But a triton snail has found it, and is killing the starfish. Unlike other animals, the snail isn't bothered by the sharp spines of the starfish.

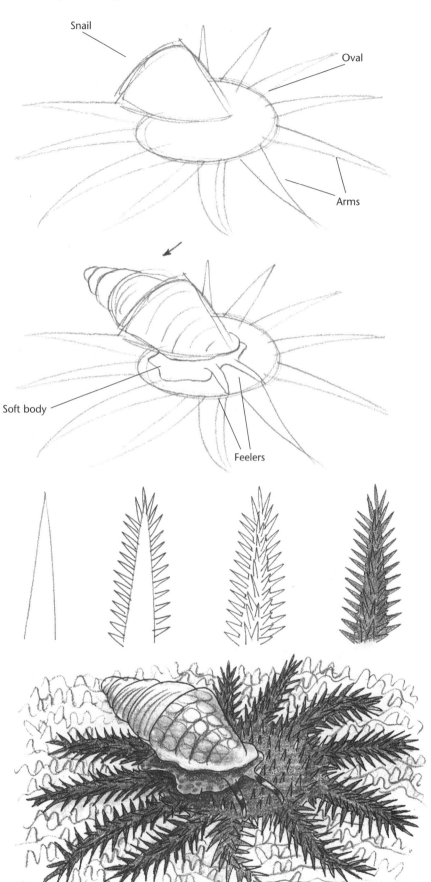

Snail

Oval

Arms

Soft body

Feelers

1. Draw the starfish as an oval, with pointed arms. Draw a triangular shape for the main part of the snail.

2. Add the back parts of the snail shell, and the soft body with feelers.

3. Complete the starfish arms by adding thorns on the outside and inside of each arm (I used a fine marker). Shade the arm gray, so the black thorns still show.

4. Draw light squiggly lines for the coral.

   Add shading and details to the snail. Clean up any smudges with your eraser.

Snail eating starfish eating coral–chow time!

Octopus

Class *Cephalopoda,* genus *Octopus.* Mollusk with eight tentacles, or arms, with suction cups. Related to squid, cuttlefish, and nautilus, an octopus has no bones. It moves by squirting water out of the siphon, an opening under its head. Has three hearts, can change colors, and shoots clouds of black 'ink' in self defense. Size: varies among 50 varieties, from 8 cm (3 in) to 8.5 m (28 ft). Diet: clams, crabs, lobsters, mussels and other shellfish. Octopuses live along coasts; not just in coral reefs.

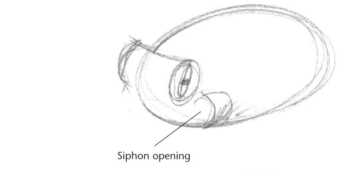

Siphon opening

1. Draw an oval for the body. Next draw a cylinder shape for the head, with an eye at the end. Add the opening for the siphon.

2. Because the octopus has no bones, the tentacles can go just about any direction. often they're curled. Draw the siphon.

   Suggestion: put tentacles curling every which way. Make a fun design!

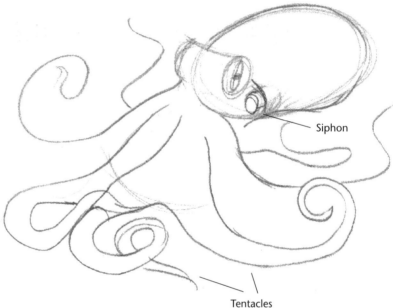

Siphon

Tentacles

3. Draw suction cups on the bottom of each tentacle. When you like the design, you can go over your final lines with a fine-tip marker. Erase the pencil lines, add shading, and clean up with an eraser.

For help finishing your drawing, see *Drawing Tips* on pages 58-62.

More Amazing Ocean Animals

Always draw lightly at first!

Tripod Fish

Bathypterois bigelowi.
Lives at depths of 3000 m (9,800 ft).
Stands on the bottom, on extended
pelvic fins and its tail, waiting for prey.

1. Start with a long, sausage-like
   body. Draw two 'legs' and the
   tail fin.

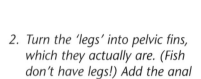

Tail fin

2. Turn the 'legs' into pelvic fins,
   which they actually are. (Fish
   don't have legs!) Add the anal
   fin.

Anal fin

Pelvic fins

3. Draw long, curving pectoral
   fins above the body. Add
   mouth and eye.

Pectoral fins

4. Add shading. Sharpen
   outlines and details. Clean up
   any smudges with your eraser.

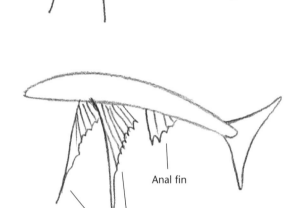

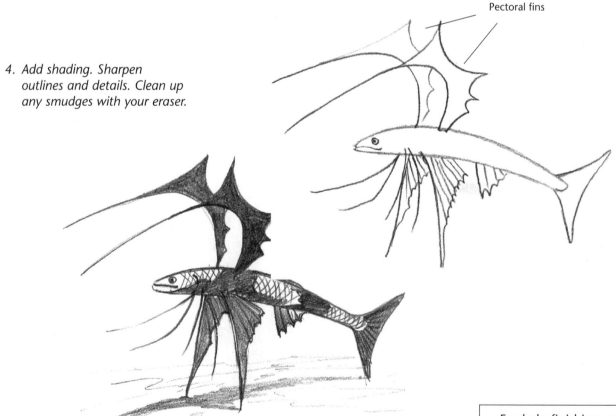

For help finishing your
drawing, see *Drawing
Tips* on pages 58-62.

44   Draw Ocean Animals

Flyingfish

Cypselurus heterurus (Atlantic flyingfish). Size: 30-43 cm (12-17 in). Diet: fish. Building up speed under water, flyingfish jump clear of the surface and extend their pectoral fins, which lie against the body when swimming. With lift from these 'wings,' they can glide for 10 seconds or so, covering 90 m (300 ft) at 1.5 m (5 ft) above the surface. Why? Most likely to escape swimming predators.

1. Start with a long, curved, flat oval for the body. Add mouth, eye, and gills.

2. Add the tail fins, with the lower one longer than the upper. Draw the dorsal, pelvic, and anal fins.

3. Draw the pectoral 'wings.' Add lines to the fins.

4. Flyingfish are fully scaled. Add shading, and scales (see Drawing Tips *at the end of the book for ideas about drawing scales). Sharpen outlines and details. Clean up with your eraser.*

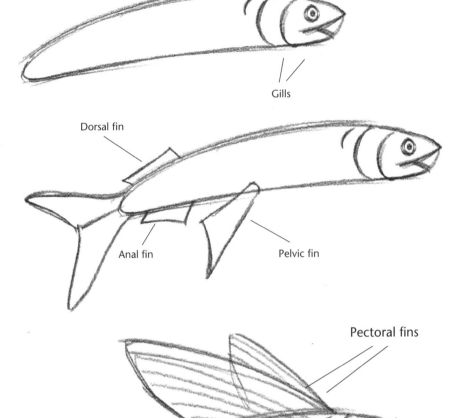

Gills

Dorsal fin

Anal fin

Pelvic fin

Pectoral fins

Angler 1

Lophius piscatorius.
Size: 1-2 m (3-6 ft). Diet: fish. Unusual flat coastal fish lies on the bottom, waiting for prey. The fringes at the edge of the body help conceal its outline. When it opens its huge mouth, its prey is sucked in with a large quantity of water. The water gets back out. The unfortunate prey stays in.

1. Draw a flat oval, with an arc across the top of it for the center line of the fish's body. Draw the rough outline of the tail–lightly!

2. Along the centerline (start far enough back to leave room for the mouth!) draw the 'fishing rod' and other dorsal spines. Add the pectoral fins and tail details.

3. Draw the mouth with teeth. Add eyes. Draw lightly at first! Now comes the part requiring patience–slowly draw the frills around the outside edge. Do a little bit at a time, erasing part of the oval as you draw.

4. Add shading. Sharpen outlines and details. Clean up any smudges with your eraser.

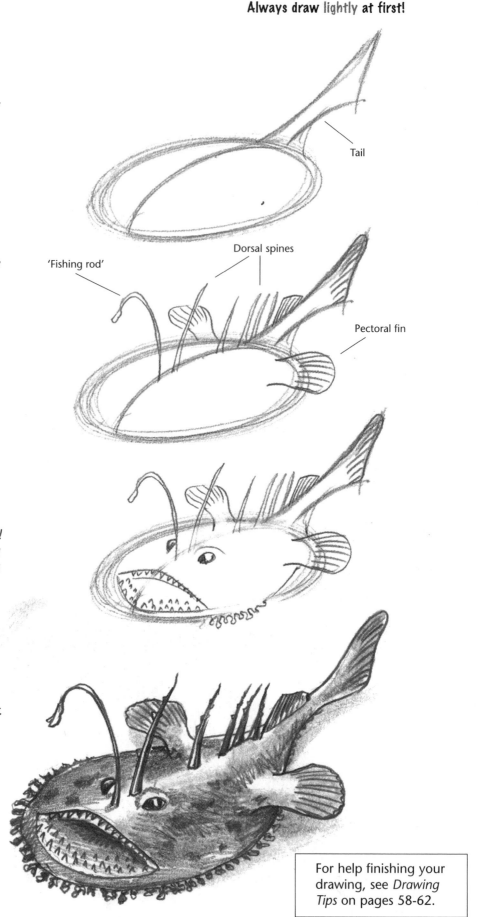

Tail

'Fishing rod'

Dorsal spines

Pectoral fin

For help finishing your drawing, see *Drawing Tips* on pages 58-62.

Always draw lightly at first!

Angler 2

Linophryne arborifera.
Size: 7 cm (3 in). This small (tiny compared to Angler 1) fish lives in the deep sea. The 'fishing rod' on its snout has a luminous lure. The chin barbel looks like a piece of seaweed. In the deep sea, where no sunlight penetrates, many animals have lights, to identify species and lure prey.

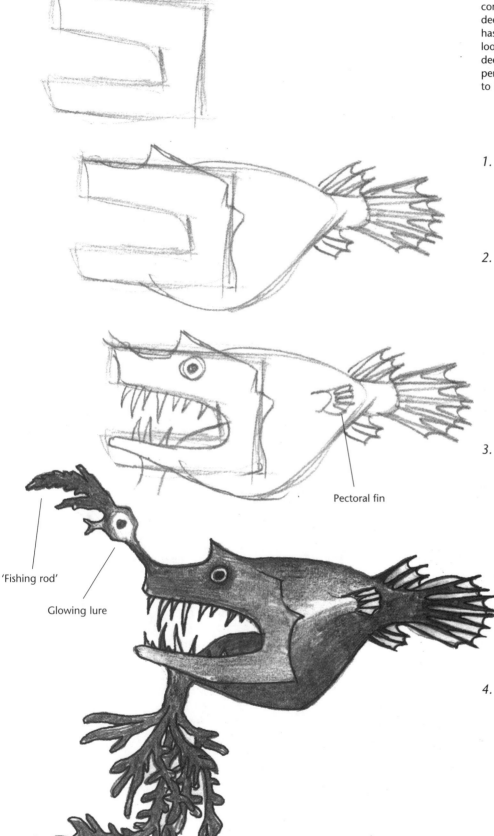

Pectoral fin

'Fishing rod'

Glowing lure

1. *Start out with a sideways U shape.*

2. *Extend the body back almost like a triangle. Add the tail, with its forked spines, plus the top and bottom fins. Draw the peak above the mouth.*

3. *Round out the mouth and add teeth (you may want to do some careful erasing first). Narrow the lower jaw as you make it rounder. Add the pectoral fin.*

4. *Add the distinctive chin barbel that looks like seaweed, and the 'fishing rod' on top with its glowing decoration. Add shading. Sharpen outlines and details. Clean up any smudges with your eraser.*

Atlantic Footballfish

Himantolophus groenlandicus.
Size: 61 cm (24 in). Diet: fish attracted
by the light in its forehead 'fishing rod.'
This deep sea angler lives 100-300 m
(330-980 ft) below the surface.

1. Start with an almost circular
   oval. Lightly divide it into four
   parts to help you place mouth
   and fins.

2. Draw the mouth. Notice that
   the front of the bottom jaw
   lines up with the centerline.
   Add teeth. Draw the eye and
   'fishing rod.'

3. Draw the remaining fins.

4. Draw the forked spines in all
   the fins, and bony plates on
   the side of the fish. Add
   shading. Sharpen outlines and
   details. Clean up any
   smudges with your eraser.

   *Congratulations! You have
   drawn one magnificently ugly
   fish.*

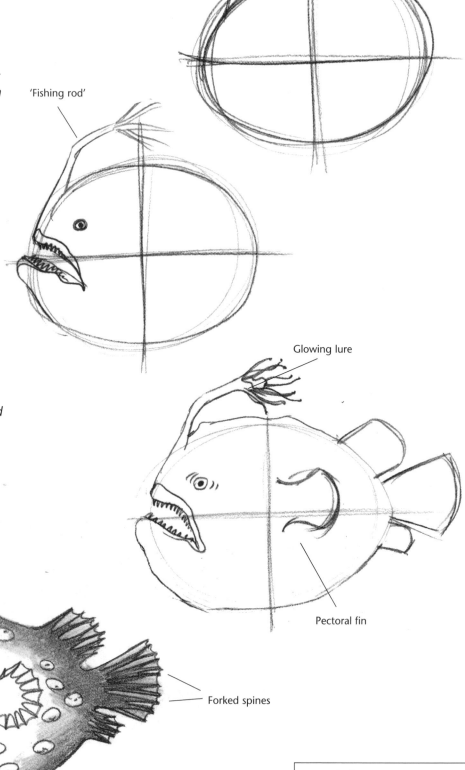

'Fishing rod'

Glowing lure

Pectoral fin

Forked spines

For help finishing your
drawing, see *Drawing
Tips* on pages 58-62.

48 Draw Ocean Animals

Always draw lightly at first!

Gulper Eel

Eurypharynx pelecanoides.
Size: 61 cm (24 in). Diet: fish, crustaceans. Another deep sea fish. Lives at 1,400 m (4,500 ft) and below. Can feed on quite large fish even though it's not much of a swimmer. Thought to swim slowly with its mouth open catching whatever it can.

1. Start with a curvy ribbon (see moray eel on pages 38-39 if you're not sure how to do this). Extend the bottom line and add the eye.

2. Next draw the mouth, a sideways 'V.' Curve the lower jaw up behind the mouth. Continue that line below the curve of the tail.

3. Add the inside section of the mouth. Drawing the remaining sections of the tail and fin can be confusing. I've tinted the part that is already drawn. The areas that aren't tinted are the parts you need to add now. Draw them.

4. Add lines on the fins, and shading. Sharpen outlines and details. Clean up any smudges with your eraser.

Squid

Loliginidae family. A mollusk related to octopus, cuttlefish, nautilus. Size: Many varieties, ranging from less than 30 cm (1 ft) to 12 m (40 ft). Diet: fish, caught with suction cups on its ten arms. Two arms are longer, and used for drawing caught prey to the mouth. Squid move by jet propulsion, filling their body with water then shooting it out. They create clouds of 'ink' to confuse predators and escape.

1. Start with a rectangle and a slightly larger triangle.

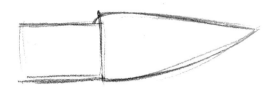

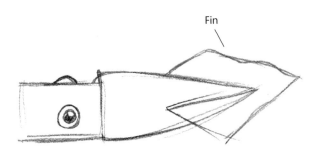
Fin

2. Draw the eye looking toward you, and the little bit you can see of the other eye. Add the fins.

Tentacles

3. Add the tentacles. Two of them are longer, with little 'paddles' on the end.

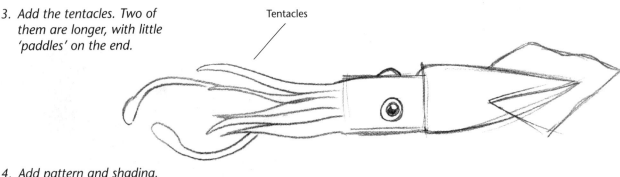

4. Add pattern and shading. Sharpen outlines and details. Clean up any smudges with your eraser.

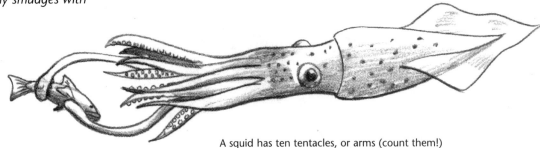

A squid has ten tentacles, or arms (count them!)

Cuttlefish

Sepia officinalis (common cuttlefish). A mollusk related to octopus and squid. Can change color at will. Grab their prey with suction cups at the end of two long tentacles. They draw it into their beak, then inject it with poison.

1. Start with an oval, surrounded by the 'wings' the cuttlefish uses to swim.

2. Draw one eye looking straight toward you. Draw the other eye, noticing that you only see the side of it. To help you draw the shorter tentacles the same length, you can draw a light arc.

3. Add eight short tentacles and two longer ones.

4. Add patterns and shading. Sharpen outlines and details. Clean up any smudges with your eraser.

Tentacles

For help finishing your drawing, see *Drawing Tips* on pages 58-62.

Porcupinefish

Diodon hystrix.
Size: 90 cm (35 in). Diet: crabs, mollusks, sea urchins. This fish has a most unusual defense—when threatened, it puffs itself up into an almost round ball, with spines sticking out all over!

1. Draw a flat oval. Add the mouth, which sticks out. Draw the eye. Add the two parts for the tail.

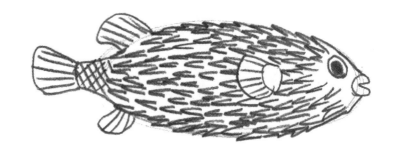

2. Add fins, with lines in them.

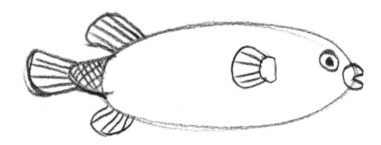

3. Draw spikes. They all point backwards when the porcupinefish is deflated.

4. If you want to draw the fish expanded, do the same drawing, only this time starting with a circle.

5. When expanded, the spines stick out from the center. I've drawn a few. You'll want to keep going until you've drawn them all.

52 Draw Ocean Animals

Always draw lightly at first!

Swordfish

Xiphias gladius.
Size: 2-5 m (6.5-16 ft). Diet: small fish, squid. Function of the 'sword' isn't clear; it may be for striking at schooling fish or just to help the swordfish swim faster. This is a very fast fish!

Sword

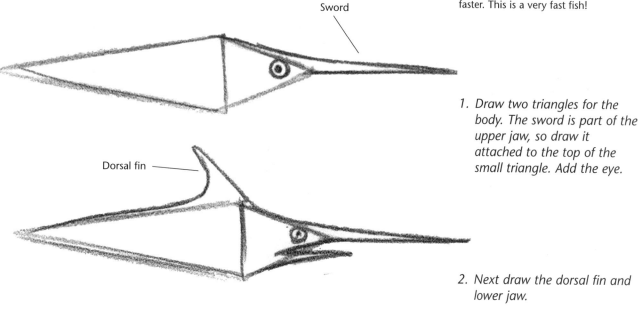

1. Draw two triangles for the body. The sword is part of the upper jaw, so draw it attached to the top of the small triangle. Add the eye.

Dorsal fin

2. Next draw the dorsal fin and lower jaw.

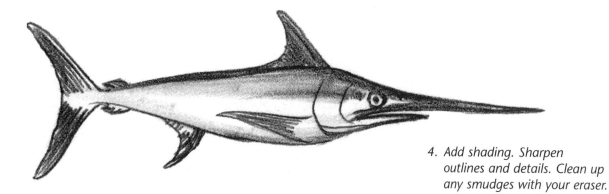

Pectoral fin

3. Add the other fins and round out the body shape.

4. Add shading. Sharpen outlines and details. Clean up any smudges with your eraser.

For help finishing your drawing, see *Drawing Tips* on pages 58-62.

Green Turtle

Chelonia mydas. Size: 1-1.5 m (3-4 ft).
Diet: sea grasses and seaweed, some
jellyfish and crustaceans. Endangered.

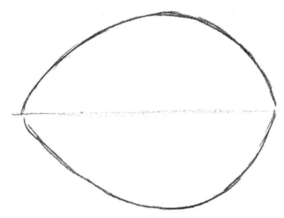

1. *Draw the outside of the shell, with center line.*

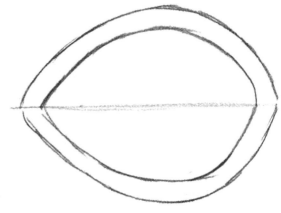

2. *Draw the same shape inside the shell.*

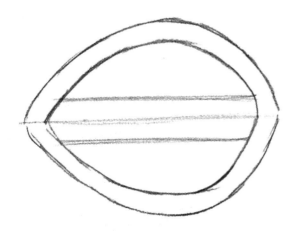

3. *Draw a line either side of the center line.*

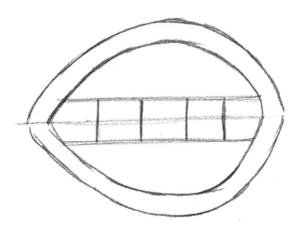

4. *Divide the center into five spaces.*

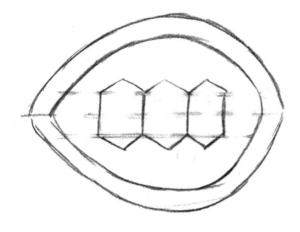

5. *Turn the middle three spaces into hexagons.*

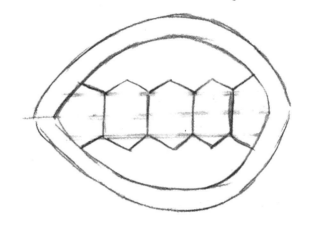

6. *Draw lines for the front and back segments.*

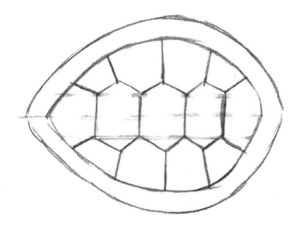

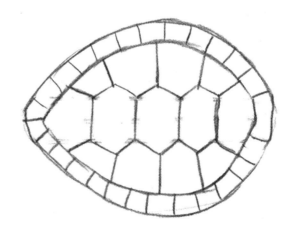

7. Draw radiating lines from the hexagon points.

8. Make lots of little segments on the outside rim. Now the hard part is done!

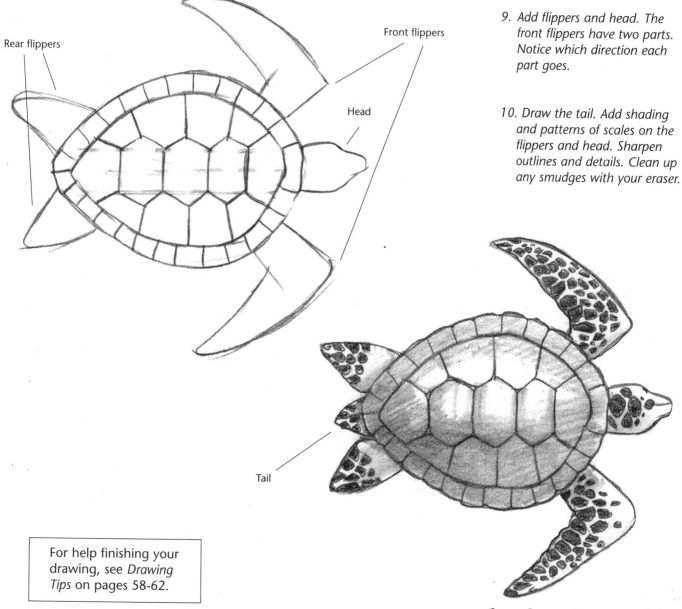

Rear flippers

Front flippers

Head

Tail

9. Add flippers and head. The front flippers have two parts. Notice which direction each part goes.

10. Draw the tail. Add shading and patterns of scales on the flippers and head. Sharpen outlines and details. Clean up any smudges with your eraser.

For help finishing your drawing, see *Drawing Tips* on pages 58-62.

California Halibut

Paralichthys californicus.
Size: 1.5 m (5 ft). Diet: fish, particularly anchovies. Is in turn eaten by rays, sea lions, porpoises and people. Like the 500 or so other species of flatfishes, young halibut swim like normal fish, with an eye on either side of their head. As they develop, one eye moves to the other side of the head. From then on, the fish swims on its side, with its eyes facing up. Flatfishes are bottom feeders.

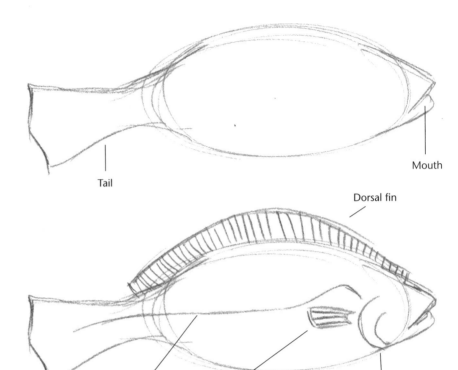

Tail

Mouth

1. Draw an oval, with one end pointed. Draw the mouth. Add the tail.

Dorsal fin

Lateral line

Pectoral fin

Gill openings

2. Draw the dorsal fin with spines. Draw the lateral line, pectoral fin and gill openings.

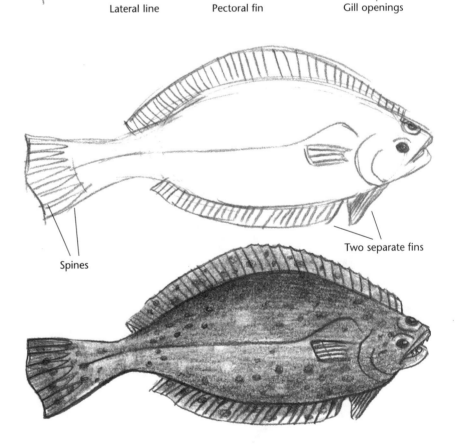

3. Add the two separate fins on the bottom. Draw the eyes and spines in tail. Lightly erase lines you don't need.

Spines

Two separate fins

4. Add shading and spots. Sharpen outlines and details. Clean up any smudges with your eraser.

For help finishing your drawing, see *Drawing Tips* on pages 58-62.

Drawing Tips

Always draw lightly at first!

Drawing Tips

Always draw lightly at first!

Scales and fins

1 Start with your basic outline.

2 Add lines in the fins.

3 Make a 'checkerboard' with diagonal lines.

4 Round edges of diamond shapes to make scales.

Always draw lightly at first!

Drawing Tips

Contour scales

It's not easy drawing scales evenly, but with a little practice, this technique might work well for you.

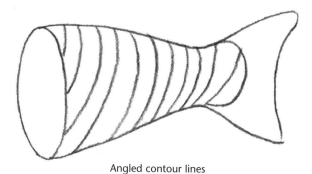

Angled contour lines

1. *Draw angled contour lines around the fish (not vertical contour lines).*

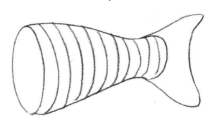

Vertical contour lines—not
what you want

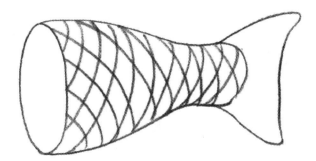

Angled contour lines going the other way

2. *Draw angled contour lines in the other direction, as evenly spaced as possible.*

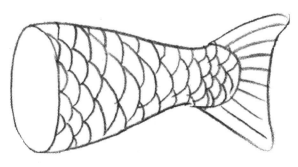

Scales!

3. *Carefully turn each small diamond shape into a scale shape. This will take some practice, but the results can be very impressive!*

Drawing Tips

Contours

1. *Here's the outline of the moray eel from page 39. Because of the way it's drawn, the eel appears to be swimming toward you.*

   Now let's shade it.

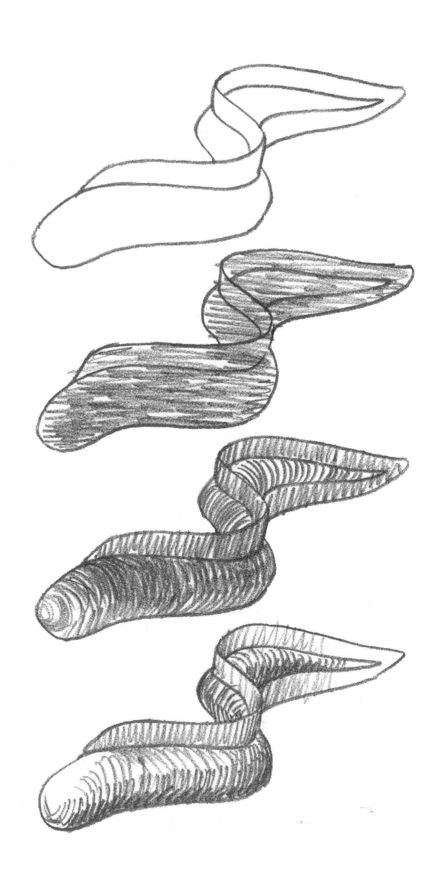

2. *Just 'coloring' it with a pencil works, but you can do better. Here I've shaded the lazy way, using just back-and-forth lines.*

3. *A more effective approach: imagine the contours of the form—how the sides curve—and try to draw your shading lines so they follow the contours.*

4. *One step better is to think about light as you follow the contours. Make the top of the form a little lighter than the bottom. Can you see the difference, with the light and dark areas?*

Drawing Tips

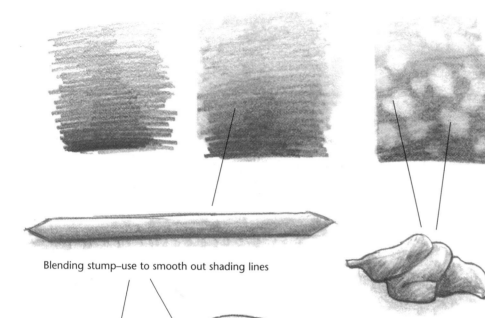

Shading

Sometimes the effect you want is a very smooth surface, with no contour lines showing on it. When that's the case, try using a blending stump.

First, carefully shade, trying not to make any obvious lines.

Next, blend the pencil marks with a blending stump (or a piece of paper or paper towel, or even your finger–that's kind of messy, though…).

Finally, use your eraser to add highlights and clean up any smudges. This technique may take some practice, but it's worth it!

Blending stump–use to smooth out shading lines

Eraser (kneadable type)–use to add highlights and clean up smudges, edges

Contour patterns

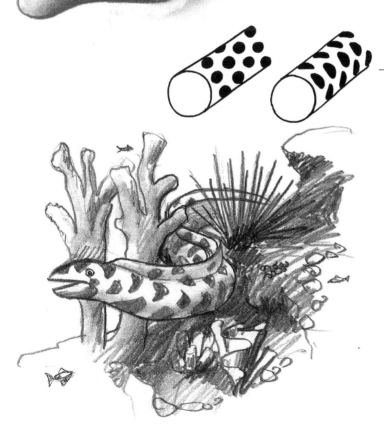

Look at these two cylinders with spots on them. Which looks rounder? Why?

Notice that I've carefully drawn the pattern so that it appears to wrap around the right cylinder. When you add patterns to your drawings of ocean animals, look for ways to make the patterns 'bend' around the animal to show its form.

It takes practice, but it can make a big difference in your drawing!

Drawing Tips

Basic Approach

1 **Put the pieces together-lightly.** During this phase, you can change or erase mistakes as you need to.

2 **Finish the drawing.** Darken important lines, junctions, and details. Add shading and textures.

3 **Clean up.** Last step in your drawing: carefully erase any smudges.

Save your work!

Whenever you do a drawing–or even a sketch–put your initials (or autograph!) and date on it. And save it. You don't have to save it until it turns yellow and crumbles to dust, but do keep your drawings, at least for several months. Sometimes, hiding in your portfolio, they will mysteriously improve! I've seen it happen often with my own drawings, especially the ones I knew were no good at all, but kept anyway....

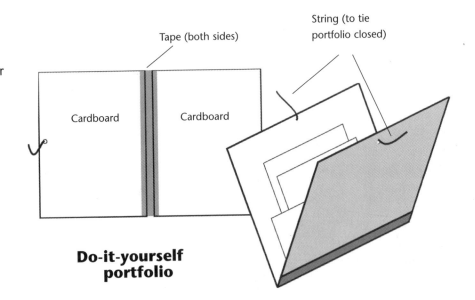

Tape (both sides)

String (to tie portfolio closed)

Cardboard   Cardboard

Do-it-yourself portfolio

Index

Learn about other books in
this series online at
www.drawbooks.com!